THE CALIFORNIA COLUMN

DURING THE CIVIL WAR

BY GEORGE HENRY PETTIS

1908

COPYRIGHT 2016 BIG BYTE BOOKS
DISCOVER MORE LOST HISTORY AT BIGBYTEBOOKS.COM

THE CALIFORNIA COLUMN

Immediately after the first battle of Bull Run, July 24th, 1861, Governor John G. Downey, of California, received from the Secretary of War, Simon Cameron, a communication which said: "The War Department accepts, for three years, one regiment of infantry and five companies of cavalry, to guard the Overland Mail Route, from Carson Valley to Salt Lake City and Fort Laramie." This was the first official action towards organizing troops in California, and it required but a short time to raise the required number of men and as fast as the companies were mustered in, at the Presidio, near San Francisco, they were transported across the bay, to Camp Downey, near where are now located the railroad shops, eastward of the Mole. In the meantime the government at Washington had an insane idea of preparing an army, on the Pacific, to be composed principally of regulars, then stationed on the coast, and under the command of General E. V. Sumner, who was in command of the Department of California, then ship them down the coast, to Mazatlan, where they were to disembark, and proceed overland, "to western Texas, and regain the public property in that state, and draw off insurgent troops from Arkansas, Missouri, etc." This movement was not to General Sumner's taste, although the governor had been directed to organize four more regiments of infantry, and one of cavalry, to take the place of the regular troops that were to go on the Texas raid.

The First Infantry, with the battalion—five companies of the First Cavalry—were being well drilled and disciplined at Camp Downey, when news was received at Department Headquarters, that the Secessionists in the south part of the state were becoming turbulent, and more outspoken and on September 17th. General Sumner ordered Colonel Carleton's command to Southern California. The Texas raid was countermanded by the Washington authorities and an order was issued for all the regulars to be sent by steamer to New York, as soon as they could be relieved by the volunteers, which movement was immediately undertaken.

The First California Infantry, under Colonel James It. Carleton, and the First California Cavalry, under Lieutenant Colonel Benjamin

F. Davis, of the First U. S. Dragoons, had arrived at San Pedro, the sea-port of Los Angeles, and had marched some eighteen miles north of that village, and laid out a camp for fifteen companies, near a small creek, about three miles east of where Santa Monica now is, and called it Camp Latham in honor of one of the senators from the state. When the order came for the relief of the regular troops, Major Edwin A. Riggs, of the First California Infantry, was sent with several companies, to Fort Yuma. Some of the regulars were at Los Angeles, (at which point Captain Winfield Scott Hancock, afterwards Major General, was on duty as Captain and Assistant Quartermaster), some of the regulars were at San Bernardino, and others were at San Diego. They were, however, all soon relieved, and rendezvoused at San Pedro for shipment to New York.

The secession element in Southern California, upon the arrival of the volunteers, became less violent, and the effect of their arrival was salutary. On the 20th of October, General E. V. Sumner was relieved of the command of the Department of California, by Colonel George Wright, of the Twelfth U. S. Infantry. Colonel Sumner was lost on the steamer Brother Jonathan, en route to Oregon. Some weeks later Colonel Wright was anxious for authority to throw troops into the State of Sonora, and indited several letters to the War Department for this purpose. November 20th, Colonel Carleton was called to San Francisco for the purpose of proceeding to and taking command of the troops on the overland route via Salt Lake City. While there, news was received of the invasion of New Mexico and Arizona, by General S. H. Sibley, with Texas troops. Wright and Carleton consulted on a plan to proceed with a command through Arizona, and attack Sibley on his flank and rear. General Wright made this matter a subject of a communication to the War Department, under date of December 9th, 1861, in which he urged the importance of the movement and its feasibility, and at the same time, he reiterated the necessity of putting troops into Sonora. The latter proposition never received any support from the authorities at Washington, but, the movement through Arizona was immediately approved, and authorized by General McClellan, as soon as it was submitted to him. About this time, a number of prominent secessionists, who were anxious to go east, and show their devotion to the cause of the rebellion, organized a party in Southern California, and with one "Dan. Showalter" at their head, attempted to get out of the State, but were captured by a detachment of the First Infantry, and were taken, bag and baggage, and landed in Fort Yuma. Although this made a great deal of talk and noise at the time, the persons in sympathy with the rebellion throughout the State announcing that it was an infringement on the constitutional rights of the citizens to molest them when they were quietly proceeding along the highways, but these fellows were caught in the chaparral, a long way from the road or trail, where they were trying to avoid the troops. Their incarceration was approved by the war department.

The movement against the rebels, under Sibley, having been approved, Fort Yuma was made the starting point of the expedition, and troops were forwarded to that place with all promptitude, an intermediate camp having been made at. Warner's Ranch, (a point about half way between Los Angeles and Fort Yuma), which was named "Camp Wright," in honor of the General commanding the Department. Supplies were being rapidly pushed forward, both by teams across the Colorado Desert, as well as by water up the Gulf of California and the Colorado River.

The California Column originally consisted of the First California Infantry, ten companies, under the command of Colonel James H. Carleton; First California Cavalry five companies, under command of Lieutenant Colonel E. E. Eyre. Lieutenant Colonel Davis having resigned and gone east, and who was killed at Beverly Ford. Virginia, June 9th, 1863; Light Battery A, Third F. S. Artillery, under the command of Lieutenant John B. Shinn, and Company B, Second California Cavalry, under the command of Captain John C. Cremoney. This command contained fifteen hundred men, well drilled, well disciplined, and all eager to show what stuff they were made of. Later on the Fifth California Infantry, under command of Colonel George W. Bowie, was added, which brought the command up to about 2,350 men, rank and file. The advance guard' or detachment, left "Camp Latham" last, and consisted of Company C, Captain McMullin, and TC, Captain Nicholas S. Davis, First Infantry, and Company B, Captain Charles A. Smith, and Company

G, Captain Hugh L. Hinds, Fifth Infantry, and followed the route of those in the advance, to "Camp Wright."

While these movements of the California troops were being made, General H. S. Sibley had arrived in New Mexico, with about 3.000 men, and had relieved Colonel Baylor from command. Colonel John R. Baylor had arrived in the territory about the 1st of July, 1801, with several hundred men of his regiment, the "Second Texas Mounted Rifles. Confederate States Army," and had announced himself as the Provisional Governor of New Mexico and Arizona.

On July 25th, Major Isaac Lynde, 7th U. S. Infantry, who was in command of Fort Fillmore, which was about three miles east of La Mesilla, and all the Union forces south of the "Tornado del Muerto," proceeded to attack Baylor's forces at La Mesilla, and after a desultory assault upon the village, he (Lynde) in the most cowardly manner, returned to the adobe walls of Fort Fillmore, having had three men killed, and two officers and four men wounded. On the morning of the 27th, Lynde vacated the fort, and commenced a retreat for Fort Stanton, having over five hundred men well equipped, armed and officered. As soon as Baylor learned of Lynde's flight, lie pursued him, with less than three hundred poorly armed men, and overtaking him near San Agustin Springs, captured the whole party, which consisted of seven companies of the 7th U. S. Infantry, and three companies of the U. S. Mounted Rifles, without firing a shot. About this time, an independent company of rebels was formed under the command of a Captain Hunter, who was ordered to proceed to Tucson, and operate down the Gila river as far as Fort Yuma. Sibley had, soon after his arrival in the territory, gone up the Rio Grande to find General Can-by, as the latter would not go down the river, and finding Fort Craig too strong to attack, had avoided it, and crossed the river to the easterly side within two miles and in plain sight of Craig. His attempting to reach the river again to get water for his men and stock at Valverde, just above the "Mesa de la Contedera," brought on the sanguinary struggle at Valverde, which took place on the 21st of February, 1862, and which was precipitated by that gallant soldier and estimable gentleman. Colonel Benjamin S. Roberts, United States Army.

Early in April, the scouts brought in news to Fort Yuma, that the rebels had left Tucson and were on their way down the Gila river, having captured Captain William McCleave and nine of his Company A. 1st Cavalry, who were scouting at White's Mills, near the Pima Villages; and sent them as prisoners to the Rio Grande. McCleave was soon paroled and returned to the column. A command under Captain William Calloway, consisting of his own Company I, 1st Infantry, a detachment of Company Av 1st Cavalry, commanded by Lieutenant -lames Barrett, with Lieutenant E. C. Baldwin, Company D, 1st Cavalry, and a detachment of Company K, 1st Infantry, under Lieutenant Jeremiah Phelan, with two mountain howitzers, were sent out from Fort Yuma, to proceed along the Overland Mail Route, with Tucson as the objective point. This command reached the Pima villages with no other signs of the rebels, than a number of burned hay stacks along the way and in due time started from that point for Tucson. When they were approaching the Picacho Peak the Indian scouts brought in information that a detachment of the rebels was in the immediate front. The detachment was ordered to make a wide detour, so as to strike them in the flank, while Calloway, with the main party, were to attack in front. The enemy were not found in the immediate front, but after traveling several miles, on April loth, 1863, rapid firing was heard in advance, and arriving upon the spot it was found that Lieutenant Barrett had located the rebels picket, and the first, intimation they had of results was that Lieutenant Barrett and two men were killed, and three were wounded. The rebel loss was two men wounded, and three were taken prisoners. The graves of the killed, the Union Lieutenant and the men, may now be seen within twenty feet of the California Southern Pacific Railroad, as it goes through Picacho Pass. The Union force bivouacked on the ground that night, and the next day, Calloway having lost his head, ordered a return to be made, against the protests of all his officers. This party was met near Stanwix Station by Colonel West and the "advance detachment" and all proceeded forward to the Pima villages.

A permanent camp was established at the Pima villages and an earth work was thrown up about the flour mill of Am mi White, who had been carried away, a prisoner, by the rebels a few weeks before. This earth work was named Fort Barrett, in honor of the lieutenant who had been killed in the skirmish at the Picacho Pass. It required several weeks for the "Column" to get to this point, as only detachments of not over four companies could move over the route through Southern California and through the entire length of Arizona, within twenty-four hours of each other, on account of the scarcity of water. On the 15th of Alay, Colonel West and his advance detachment moved out of the Pima villages for Tucson. They left the overland route at the Sacatone Station, going via White's Ranch, through the Casas Grandes, Rattlesnake Springs, and arrived at old Fort Breckenridge, near the confluence of the Gila and San Pedro rivers, where the American flag was run up again, on the flag staff of the fort, amid the hurrahs of the men, and the field music playing the "Star Spangled Banner" At this point the Pima Indian herders, who had been employed to drive along the livestock of the command, and some others who had been employed as scouts, refused to go any further, and demanded their pay of the quartermaster. They asserted that the command was too small to take Tucson; that they were greatly outnumbered by the rebels, and besides, there were rifle pits fully manned, more than a mile in length to be overcome. They were allowed to return home. The command encamped that night in the Cañon de Oro. The next day. May 19th, a short march of fifteen miles was made, and the party encamped within ten miles of Tucson. An early reveille on the morning of the 20th, and the command moved forward with a light step. When it had arrived within two miles of the town, Captain Emil Fritz, Company B, 1st Cavalry was sent forward the first platoon to make a detour and come in on the east side of the town; the second platoon, under Lieutenant Juan Francisco Guirado, afterwards aide-de-camp on the staff of Brigadier General Joseph R. West, in New Mexico, and later in Arkansas and Missouri, since deceased, was to charge in on the north side, while the four companies of infantry were to move directly on the road, and come in at the west side of the town. The programme was completely carried out, as the three parties came on to the plaza of Tucson at the same moment, the cavalry at a charge, and the infantry on the double quick, but found no enemy. In fact, there was no enemy, nor were there any people, the only living things found within the limits of the town, were an unsuspected number of dogs and cats. The rebels, before they had hurriedly left, had publicly announced that the "Abs" would soon take the fair city, which would then be given over to the ravages of a brutal soldiery. The rebels retreated to the Rio Grande accompanied by a number of desperadoes, amongst whom was the notorious Judge (?) Ed [Ned] McGowan, of San Francisco, of Vigilante Days fame, who were also rebels at heart, while the Mexican population, men women and children, started southward for the Sonora line. Good quarters were found here for the troops, and it required two months' time, or until July 20th, to get the Column assembled here, with food and forage enough to make another start. Everything, except a small amount of wheat, which was purchased of the Pima Indians, was brought by teams from Southern California, via Fort Yuma, a distance of several hundred miles. Xo forage or food could be had in or about Tucson, and the men could eat nearly as much as the few trains could bring up. Xo news had been received from the Rio Grande since the column had commenced its march from California. Several express parties had been sent forward to open communications with General [Edward] Canby, but none had ever returned. On June loth, a party of three persons, consisting of Sergeant William Wheeling, Company F, 1st Infantry, expressman John Jones, and a Mexican guide named Chaves, left Tucson with dispatches for General Canby, written on tissue paper. It was afterwards learned that this party was attacked by Apache Indians as they were emerging out of the Apache Pass, on the 18th: Chaves was killed at the first fire and Sergeant Wheeling was seriously wounded, he soon fell from his horse, and was immediately dispatched. Their bodies were afterwards found horribly mutilated, disemboweled and spread-eagled—fires having been built over them, and were filled with arrows, after the manner of "John Apache." Years afterwards the same fate fell to Jones. Jones escaped almost by a miracle, and getting through the Indians, who followed him for a long distance, he succeeded after a ride of over two hundred miles, in reaching the Rio Grande, at Picacho a small village about five miles above

Mesilla. Here he was taken prisoner by the rebels, who brought him before Colonel William Steele, who examined him, took his dispatches, and threw him into jail. He managed, however, to get word to General Canby that he was there, and that the California Column was really coming, an achievement that was considered absolutely impracticable.

On the 21st of June, a strong reconnoitering party of cavalry, under Lieutenant Colonel Eyre, left Tucson for the Rio Grande. After a hard march they arrived at old Fort Thorn on July 4th, which they found abandoned by the rebels. Here he was reinforced by a squadron of the 3rd U. S. Cavalry, under Captain Howland, and would have proceeded to attack the rebels at Mesilla, but was obliged to forego that pleasure, by peremptory orders from Colonel Chivington, 1st Colorado Volunteers, at Fort Craig, who was in command of the southern military district of New Mexico, and who was acting under General Canby's orders, as Colonel Steele greatly feared he would be overtaken by the California troops, and in his hurried retreat burned a number of his wagons, and destroyed a large amount of ammunition. The rebel forces were so disheartened and so thoroughly disorganized, that, had they been attacked by even a small force, they would have at once surrendered.

On July 9th Captain Thomas L. Roberts with his Co. E. 1st Infantry, and Captain Cremoney's Company B, 2nd Cavalry, and two mountain howitzers, under command of Lieutenant William A. Thompson, 1st Infantry, left Tucson for Rio do Sauze, where they were to establish a camp, having with them rations and forage for Colonel Eyre's command, in case they were forced back by the Texans. When this command reached Apache Pass, (now Fort Bowie), they were attacked by a large force of Apache warriors, under the leadership of "Cochise." the Indians having possession of the water at that point. After a stubborn contest, in which both trails of the mountain howitzers were broken, in elevating the pieces to reach the Indians upon the hill where the spring was, the Indians were forced to retire, with a loss of nine killed, while the troops suffered a loss of two killed and two wounded.

On the 20th of July Colonel West, with Companies B. Captain Valentine Fresher, C, Captain William McMullin and K. Lieutenant George H. Pettis, 1st Infantry, and Company G, Captain Hugh L. Hinds,. 5th Infantry left Tucson for the Rio Grande. On the 21st, a second command consisting of Lieutenant John B. Shinn's Light Battery A. 3rd V. S. Artillery, and Company A, Captain Edward B. Willis, 1st Infantry and Company B, Captain Charles A. Smith, 6th Infantry, left Tucson for tin* same destination, under command of Captain Willis. On the 23rd, Lieutenant Colonel Edwin A. Rigg, with a third command, consisting of Companies I, Captain William Calloway, F, Captain Washington L. Parvin, D. Captain Francis S. Mitchell, and H, Captain Lafayette Hammond all of the 1st Infantry, followed. Each of these detachments had subsistence for thirty days, with a full supply of entrenching tools. Up to the time of the arrival of the troops at Tucson, the infantry had packed their knapsacks the entire march, a notable achievement, considering the nature of the country—and its lack of resources—through which they had so far marched, and the fearful heat and thirst which they had encountered.

General Orders. No. 10. "Headquarters of the Column from California, dated Tucson July 17th, 1862, contained the following paragraphs:

"10. That every soldier may move forward with a light, free step, now that we approach the enemy, he will no longer be required to carry his knapsack.

"11. This is the time when every soldier in this column looks forward with a confident hope that, he, too, will have the distinguished honor of striking a blow for the old Stars and Stripes; when he, too, feels in his heart that he is the champion of the holiest cause that has ever yet nerved the arm of a patriot. The general commanding the 'Column' desires that such a time shall be remembered by all, but more particularly by those who, from their guilt, have been so unfortunate on such an occasion. He therefore orders that all soldiers under his command, who may be held in confinement, shall be at once relieved.'"

The troops had been in Tucson for two months, from May 20th, to July 20th. After the first alarm, upon the arrival of the Union troops, scouts were sent forward towards the Sonora line, and the Mexican residents returned to their homes. A number of American desperadoes also put in an appearance. A number of these were arrested by General Carleton who in a letter to General Wright, at San Francisco, said, under date of Tucson, June 10th, 1862: II shall send to Fort Yuma, for confinement, starting them today, nine of the cut-throats, gamblers, and loafers, who have infested this town to the great bodily fear of all good citizens. Nearly everyone, I believe, has either killed his man or been engaged in helping to kill him.

Sylvester J. Mowry, of Rhode Island, who had been an officer in the U.S. Army, was living near Tucson, at the Patagonia Mine, and being an uncompromising rebel, was arrested, examined by a military commission, was sent down to Fort Yuma at this time. Tucson soon became a cleanly and model town, and the long rest here repaid the command for the many days of previous marching.

General Carleton, with headquarters of the California Column arrived at Fort Thom, on August 7th, and immediately communicated with General Canby. The balance of the "Column" arrived on the Rio Grande in detachments, as they had left Tucson, one day apart, and by the 15th, Mesilla was made the headquarters of the District of Arizona, and had as a garrison companies B, C, D and K, 1st Infantry, and Company A. 5th Infantry. Shinn's Light Battery A, 3rd U. S. Artillery, Companies A and E, 1st Infantry, B, 5th Infantry, Band D, 1st Cavalry, and B, 2nd Cavalry, were sent as a garrison to Fort Fillmore, opposite to and about three miles from Mesilla. Shinn's battery being shortly afterwards sent to the Cottonwoods about 25 miles south of Fort Fillmore, to recruit their horses. Company A, 1st Infantry, was sent to Franklin, Texas, (now El Paso), to take care of Simeon Hart's flour mill and look out for the mail carrier of the rebels—the notorious "Captain Skillman." afterwards killed by Captain Albert H. French, at Spencer's Ranch, near Presidio del Norte, April 15th, 1864, on the Rio Grande, in an attempt to carry the rebel mail into Texas. All the regular troops were soon relieved and sent up to Fort Craig, and the Californians proceeded to Forts Quitman, Bliss, and Davis, in Texas, and hauled up the Union Flag.

The Southern Overland Mail Route had been opened and the United States military posts in Arizona, Southern New Mexico, and Northwestern Texas, had been reoccupied by troops composing the California Column. General Carleton in his report to Assistant Adjutant General Drum, of the Department of California, under date of September 20th, 1862, said: "It was no fault of the troops from California that the Confederate forces fled before them. It is but just to say that their having thus fled is mainly attributed to the gallantry of the troops under General Canby's command. That they were hurried in their flight, by the timely arrival of the advance guard of the California Column under Lieutenant Colonel Eyre there cannot be a doubt. The march from the Pacific to the Rio Grande by the California Column was not accomplished without immense toil and great hardships, or without many privations and much suffering from heat and want of water."

* * * * * * * * *

"The march of the Column from California in the summer months, across the great desert in the driest season that has been known for thirty years, is a military achievement creditable to the soldiers of the American army: but it would not be just to attribute the success of this march to any ability on my part. That success was gained only by the high physical and moral energies of that peculiar class of officers and men who composed the California Column. With any other troops I am sure I should have failed.

"I send you a set of colors which have been borne by this column. They were hoisted by Colonel West over Forts Breckenridge and Buchanan, and over Tucson by Colonel Eyre over Forts Thorn and Fillmore, and over Mesilla, New Mexico; and over Fort Bliss in Texas. They were hoisted by Captain Cremoney over Fort Quitman, and by Captain Shirland over Fort Davis in Texas, and thus again have those places been consecrated to our beloved country."

On the 18th of September, 1862, General Carleton assumed command of the Department of New Mexico, General Canby having been ordered east by the War Department, the Column was soon distributed throughout the Department, and active operations commenced against the hostile Indians—the Apaches and the Navajos. Treason was at a discount in New Mexico, and no treasonable utterances were allowed; when anything of this kind was attempted, it resulted in the person being immediately arrested, confined in the guard house, and tried by a military commission. The most incorrigible of this class of persons, was Samuel J. Jones, the well-known pro-slavery sheriff at Lecompton, Kansas, in 1857 and '58. Upon the advent of Colonel Baylor's forces in 1861, he was the post sutler at Fort Fillmore, owning a fine estate at Mesilla, and during the rebel occupation of the territory he was constantly in hot water with the rebels, but not on account of political matters, however, as he was an unadulterated fire-eater [pro-secessionist]. After the Column arrived in the District of New Mexico, Jones was brought up in the guard-house about once a month upon an average.

When General Carleton assumed command of the Department of New Mexico he relinquished the immediate command of the California Column and published the following order:

Headquarters of the Department of New Mexico,

Santa Fe, N. M., Sept. 21st, 1862.

Gen. Orders No. 85.

In entering upon the duties that remove him from immediate association with the troops constituting the Column from California, the Commanding General desires to express his grateful acknowledgment of the conduct and services of the officers and men of that command. Traversing a desert country, that has heretofore been regarded as impracticable for the operations of large bodies of troops, they have reached their destination and accomplished the object assigned them, not only without loss of any kind, but improved in discipline, in morale, and in every other element of efficiency. That patient and cheerful endurance of hardships, the zeal and alacrity with which they have grappled with, and overcome obstacles that would have been insurmountable to any but troops oil the highest physical and moral energy, the complete abnegation of self, and subordination of every personal consideration, to the great object of our hopes and efforts, give the most absolute assurance of success in any field or against any enemy.

California has reason to be proud of the sons she has sent across the continent to assist in the great struggle in which our country is now engaged. The Commanding General is requested by the officer who preceded him in the command of this department, to express for him the gratification felt by every officer and soldier of his command at the fact that troops from the Atlantic and Pacific slope, from the mountains of California and Colorado, acting in the same cause, inspired by the same duties, and animated by the same hopes, have met and shaken hands in the center of this great continent.

(Signed) JAMES H. CARLETON,

Brigadier General U. S. Volunteers, Commanding Department.

During the years of '63 and '64 there were continual reports that the rebels in Texas were organizing expeditions to retake New Mexico and Arizona, which required a large force to be kept in the southern part of the territory. They were, however, kept busy against the Apaches and skirmishes were numerous, and the duty very hard on account of long distances between water. Among the memorable events in 1863, was the taking of the celebrated Apache chief Mangus Colorado (The Red Sleeve) and his being killed by Captain E. D. Shirland's Company C, 1st Cavalry. The old chief had been taken prisoner in a skirmish, and was confined in a Sibley tent at old Fort McLean, near the Mimbres river, in January, 1863. The guard had strict orders that if he attempted to escape, to shoot him. In the early morning the soldier on guard in rear of the tent, saw Mangus rise up from the tent and started to run. He raised his carbine, fired, and the scoundrel fell dead in his tracks. He had committed so many murders and outrages that the question of whether or not he really attempted to escape was never satisfactorily settled. The other event was the expedition against the Navajos, under the command of Colonel Kit Carson, and of which Captain Asa B. Carey, 13th U.S. Infantry, who was since Paymaster General of the U. S. Army but now retired, was chief commissary of subsistence, was general aid and military adviser, in which Companies B and D, 1st California Cavalry, and Companies H and K, 1st California Infantry, took part. Company G, 1st Infantry, Captain Henry A. Greene, established on July 3rd, 1863, Port McRea, at the Ojo del Muerto, about two miles west of the Tornado del Muerto, and there the captain gained much credit for his constant and repeated conflicts with the Indians. The Navajo expedition, by July, 1861, had been successful in capturing over 9,000 of the Indians, and they were taken to Fort Sumner, (Bosque Redondo) on the Pecos river, about five hundred miles from their own home. These Indians were completely whipped in to subjugation, all of their crops and plantings were destroyed, and all of their stock captured. They were taken back to their old homes in 1868, and they have never been on the war path since. A large number of the Column were stationed at Fort Sumner guarding these prisoners.

During the year 1863, there were three commissioned officers killed and four wounded; fourteen enlisted men were killed and twenty-one wounded. Three hundred and one Indians were killed, eighty-seven wounded and seven hundred and three taken prisoners. During 1864 there were the usual number of skirmishes, and the Navajo war was completed.

Some of the Column was in the celebrated Sand Creek Fight,* which took place north of the Canadian river near Bent's Old Fort. Company K, 1st Infantry and Companies D and B, 1st Cavalry, were as far east as Fort Dodge, Kansas, escorting trains). In Carson's fight with the Comanche and Kiowa Indians, November 25th, on the Canadian river, at the Adobe Walls, the Column was represented by detachments from Company B, Captain Emil Fritz, 1st Cavalry, and Company K, 1st Infantry, Lieutenant George H. Pettis. Major William McCleave, 1st Cavalry, was second in command.

Now referred to as the Sand Creek Massacre or the Chivington Massacre. On November 29, 1864, a 700-man force of Colorado Territory militia attacked and destroyed a peaceful village of Cheyenne and Arapaho in southeastern Colorado Territory, killing and mutilating an estimated 70–163 Native Americans, about two-thirds of whom were women and children.—Ed. 2016

During this year there was one commissioned officer killed, and two wounded, six enlisted men killed, and twenty-three wounded. Three hundred and sixty-three Indians were killed, one hundred and forty wounded. Eight thousand and ninety-three were taken prisoners in the Department of New Mexico.

Nine companies of the 1st California Infantry, and the five original companies of the 1st California Cavalry, were discharged in August and September, 1864, their term of service having expired. On January 20th, 1865, John Wilson, the last enlisted man of Company K, the tenth company of the 1st California Infantry, was discharged. On February 15th, Lieutenant George H. Pettis, of said Company lv, was mustered out at Santa Fe, New Mexico, by Captain Asa B. Carey, Thirteenth United States Infantry, Chief Mustering Officer, when the record of the California Column ceased.

MEMBERS

The biographical sketches of officers and enlisted men of the California Column. They are the most complete and the best obtainable at this time and the Historical Society is under great obligations to Captain George H. Pettis for his excellent work and very timely aid in securing them for the archives and publications of the society. The sketches were edited by Max Frost, treasurer of the society.

JAMES [HENRY] CARLETON

Late Brevet Major General United States Volunteers in Command.

James H. Carleton was appointed second lieutenant. First United States Dragoons, October 18, 1839; promoted to be first lieutenant March 17, 1845; promoted to be captain February 16, 1847; breveted major, February 23, 1847, for gallant and meritorious conduct at Buena Vista, Mexico, and was appointed major Sixth United States Cavalry, September 7, 1861. He was commissioned as colonel First California Infantry Volunteers and is recognized by the War Department as having been in the military service of the United States in that grade and organization from August 7, 1861. He was appointed brigadier general of the United States Volunteers April 28, 1862, which appointment he accepted on the same day; was breveted lieutenant colonel and colonel in the regular army March 13, 1865, for meritorious services in New Mexico; breveted brigadier general in the regular army on the same day for gallant and meritorious services in the Northwest and was breveted major general of the United States Volunteers on the same day for meritorious services during the war. He was honorably mustered out of the volunteer service April 30, 1860; was promoted to be lieutenant colonel, Fourth United States Cavalry, July 31, 1866. He died January 7, 1873. From October 14th, 1861, to May 15, 1862, he was in command of the district of Southern California; thence to August 14, 1862, in command of the Column from California; thence to September 5, 1862, in command of the district of Arizona; thence to September 18, 1862, in command in the field; thence to September 12, 1865, in command of the department of New Mexico;

thence to April 30, 1866, in command of the district of New Mexico. This officer stated that he was born in Eastport, Maine, but did not report to the War Department the date of his birth.

His date of birth was December 27, 1814. He married Sophia Garland Wolfe in 1848 and they had two children.—Ed. 2016

The records on file in the War Department concerning this officer are purely of a military character and contain no information relative to this officer prior to his entry into service.

General Carleton also served with his regiment while a captain in New Mexico during the years of 1855, 1856, and 1857, and engaged in numerous skirmishes and expeditions against the Apaches, Navajos and Utes. A few of the old timers still alive in the Territory remember him kindly and speak of him very highly as a gallant and successful Indian fighter.

His army record is one of the best among the officers of the "old army" before the war.

General Carleton was a Free Mason and a member of Montezuma Lodge No. 1 of that order in the City of Santa Fe and was made an Entered Apprentice April 22, 1856, a Fellow Craft April 25, 1856, and a Master Mason April 29, 1856, and remained a member of the lodge until his demitted November 24, 1860. Upon his return to Santa Fe as a commanding general of the Department of New Mexico he affiliated with Montezuma Lodge August 1, 1863, and remained a member thereof until his demise.

ASA B. CAREY

Brigadier General U. S. Army. Retired.

Is a native of the state of Connecticut, and was appointed to the West Point Military Academy from that state July 1, 1854; breveted second lieutenant Sixth U. S. Infantry-July 1, 1858; appointed second lieutenant, Seventh U.S. Infantry October 22, 1858; promoted first lieutenant Thirteenth U.S. Infantry May 14, 1861; appointed captain Thirteenth U.S. Infantry October 24, 1861; appointed major and paymaster October 5, 1867; lieutenant colonel deputy paymaster general March 27, 1895; colonel assistant paymaster general June 10, 1898; brigadier general paymaster general, January 30, 1899; retired from active service July 12, 1899.

While serving in the Seventh U.S. Infantry Lieutenant Carey marched with his regiment from Utah to New Mexico, the march consuming four months, namely: The months of May, June, July and August, 1860. The four months were full of hardships and severe duty as may well be imagined when the conditions of the country through which the regiment marched at that time are taken into consideration.

From April, 1860, to September, 1861, he participated with his company in an expedition against the Navajos in New Mexico and Arizona, under the command of Lieutenant Colonel Edward R. S. Canby, during which the command did much scouting and fighting. After the expedition returned Lieutenant Carey served as depot quartermaster at Albuquerque, then as depot quartermaster at Fort Union during the winter of 1861-62.

In March and April, 1862, he was in command of two companies of infantry and a battery of mountain howitzers which command formed a part of the force under the command of Major J. M. Chivington, which attacked the rear guard of the Confederates constituted of Texas volunteers at the battle of Apache Pass, or Glorieta, March 28, 1862. The battalion under the command of the then Captain Carey captured the rear guard of the Confederates, and destroyed the enemy's train and supplies of every kind. This brilliant feat of arms compelled the Confederates to retire in a hurry upon their base of supplies in Santa Fe, the capital, about twenty-five miles to the south of Apache Pass. From there the Confederate force under the command of General Sibley retired south towards Texas, and evacuated the northern part of New Mexico. Captain Carey was then ordered back to Fort Union, and resumed duty as depot commissary and quartermaster at that fort.

Upon the creation of the eastern district of New Mexico he was appointed to the command of all the troops in the district, which contained all of the Territory of New Mexico east of the Pecos river, with headquarters at Fort Union.

Indians were plentiful and warlike. A number of successful expeditions by the troops under his command occurred at various dates during the time lie was the commanding officer.

He was then assigned to duty as chief quartermaster in the 1863 campaign against the hostile Navajos and Apaches under the command of Colonel Christopher Car-son, afterwards brigadier general U. S. Volunteers, and was with General Carson's force until May 1864. He was detailed by General Carson, who had been promoted to brigadier general, to take the first detachment of Navajo prisoners and locate them on the reservation set apart for them at Fort Sumner, on the Pecos river. Part of the time he was also in command of the expeditionary force, in the Navajo campaign, which transported over 9,000 Navajo prisoners, men, women and children from their reservation in western New Mexico and eastern Arizona to their new reservation at Fort Sumner, on the Pecos river.

After the close of the Navajo campaign he served as chief quartermaster of the Department of New Mexico, with headquarters in Santa Fe. During the winter of 1864-65 he was assigned to duty as chief mustering officer for the Department of New Mexico, and in that capacity had charge of the mustering out of all of the U. S. volunteers, consisting of New Mexico Infantry and Cavalry regiments, and California Infantry and Cavalry regiments. After the close of the war ho was ordered to Washington to settle his accounts.

After his appointment as major and paymaster he performed another tour of duty in Few Mexico, namely: as chief paymaster of the district of New Mexico, stationed at Santa Fe. This, however, was not as arduous and as dangerous as his tours of duty in Indian campaigns, and against the Confederate forces commanded by General Sibley.

He was stationed in the city of Santa Fe as chief paymaster from 1868 to 1874, and thereafter ordered to duty in the office of the paymaster general in Washington, which closed his military career in the Sunshine Territory.

He was breveted major for conspicuous gallantry at the battle of Apache Pass, March 28, 1862. Also breveted lieutenant colonel for gallant and meritorious services in the war with the hostile Navajo Indians.

Retired by operation of law July 12, 1899, with the rank of brigadier general and paymaster general of the army.

General Carey made a gallant record during his six years of service in this Territory, and justly attained the reputation of a very meritorious officer and able commander. Many of the old soldiers still alive in New Mexico remember him fondly and kindly, at the date of this, March 1st, 1908.

WILLIAM LOGAN RYNERSON

Late Captain First California Volunteer Infantry and Captain and Assistant Quartermaster United States Volunteers.

William Logan Rynerson was born in Hardin county, Kentucky, a few miles from the birthplace of Abraham Lincoln, the martyred president of the United States, in 1836 [sic, February 22, 1828]. He was raised on a farm and in early life engaged in the raising of blooded horses and cattle. In the latter fifties the California fever seized him and he emigrated to the then Land of Gold, tramping it across the plains and mountains of Nebraska, Utah and Nevada. The hardships were many but he stood them manfully.

He then engaged in joining and for a while managed a butcher shop in one of the mining camps, studying law at the same time.

When the First California Volunteer Infantry was organized at San Francisco he enlisted and was made first sergeant of Company C of the regiment, January 1st, 1862. He was promoted to second lieutenant of Company B, of the regiment, vice Second Lieutenant George H. Pettis, promoted, February 5, 1862.

April 16, 1862, he was promoted to first lieutenant of Company B, of the same regiment. He was appointed adjutant of the regiment shortly thereafter and served faithfully and efficiently in that capacity until August 9, 1864, when he received a captaincy in the regiment.

Early in 1865 he was transferred to the staff as captain and assistant quartermaster of volunteers and served as such until mustered out in 1866. Upon his muster out he settled in Mesilla, Dona Ana county, shortly thereafter moving to Las Cruces, the town then started two miles north of Mesilla.

He was admitted to the bar and commenced the practice of law in Las Cruces.

While in Santa Fe, serving as a member of the legislative assembly from the county of Dona Ana, an altercation ensued between him and Chief Justice John D. Slough of the Supreme Court of New Mexico. Judge Slough had been a colonel in command of the regiment of Colorado Volunteers that participated in the battle of Apache Pass or Glorieta, March 28, 1862.

The Battle of Apache Pass was actually July 15–16, 1862.—Ed. 2016

Judge Slough and Colonel Rynerson, the latter having since been breveted as colonel of volunteers for gallant and meritorious services during the war, were both fearless and brave men. Judge Slough while in the billiard room of the Fonda Hotel, then the principal stopping place and leading caravan-serai between Kansas City and West Port, in Missouri, and San Francisco, California, made very bitter and slurring remarks concerning Colonel Rynerson which were reported to the latter. In those days everybody who could afford it in the Southwest carried a pistol. Colonel Rynerson went to the Fonda, called upon Judge Slough to retract and as the story goes, Judge Slough instead of doing so endeavored to put his hand behind his back, to draw a Derringer he carried. At that moment Colonel Rynerson pulled his pistol and shot him dead. This happened on the 15 day of December, 1867.

There was testimony adduced to the fact that Judge Slough had a Derringer pistol in his hand, which he put behind his back.

A coroner's jury investigated the affair and fully exonerated Colonel Rynerson. Thereafter Colonel Rynerson became a prominent citizen. He was an influential politician and enjoyed a good practice as a lawyer until the time of his death which occurred July 4, 1893 [*sic*, September 23, 1893].

He was prominent in the Masonic order and attained the thirty-second degree of Scottish Rite Free Masonry and had served the Grand Lodge of New Mexico as second Grand Master in 1879. He - was also a member of Santa Fe Chapter No. 1, Royal Arch Masons and of Santa Fe Commandery No. 1, Knights Templar. He had attained a 32nd degree Master of the Royal Secret, in the Ancient and Accepted Scottish Rite of Freemasonry, for the Southern Jurisdiction of the United States; was a member of the Santa Fe Lodge of Perfection No. 1.

He was a member of the constitutional convention of New Mexico in 1889 and had served several times as territorial district attorney of his district and as a member of the legislative council and the House of Representatives of the New Mexico assembly.

As a man, as a citizen, as an official and as a soldier he made a splendid record. In the Masonic fraternity he assumed a high position on account of his loyalty and zeal as a Free Mason. His remains "were buried with Masonic honors in the Masonic cemetery at Las Cruces.

GEORGE HENRY PETTIS

Brevet Captain United States Volunteers, First Lieutenant Company K, First California Volunteer Infantry.

George Henry Pettis was born at Pawtucket, R. I., March 17th, 1831; at the age of twelve years entered the office of the *Advertiser*, a newspaper published at Cohoes, New York; in 1849 removed to Providence, R. I., where lie followed the occupation of printer until 1854, when he went to California, arriving at San Francisco on June 17th, of that year, on the steamer *Brother Jonathan*, via Nicaragua; he was engaged in mining in the vicinity of Garrote, Tuolumne county, from June, 1854, until May, 1858, when he arrived at San Francisco en route to Frazer river. The Frazer river bubble having collapsed he resumed his occupation as a printer, and was employed upon the *Alta California* and the *Morning Call*, and held a situation on the *Herald*. When President Lincoln made a call upon California for troops, he entered the military service of the United States as Second Lieutenant, Company B, 1st California Infantry. He was promoted to First Lieutenant, Company Iv, same regiment, January 1st, 1862, commanding the company nearly all of the time, until mustered out on February 15th 1865, when he was immediately mustered into the service again as First Lieutenant, Company F. 1st New Mexico Volunteer Infantry, Colonel Francisco Paula Abreu. He commanded Company F until promoted to Adjutant of the regiment, June 1st, 1865, and was finally mustered out, his services being no longer required, September 1st, 1866, having served continuously for five years and fifteen days. He was in a number of skirmishes with Apache and Navajo Indians; breveted Captain U. S. Volunteers, March 13th, 1865, "for distinguished gallantry in the engagement at the Adobe Walls, Texas, with the Comanche and Kiowa Indians," November 25th, 1864, in which he commanded the Artillery.

In 1868, he removed from New Mexico to Providence. R. I.; was a member of the Common Council, from the Ninth Ward, from June, 1872, to January 1876 and a member of the Rhode Island House of Representatives in 1876 and 1877: was Boarding Officer of the port of Providence from 1878 to 1885; was marine editor of the *Providence Journal* from 1885 to 1887; Sealer of Weights and Measures and Superintendent of Street Signs and Numbers at Providence, Rhode Island from March 10th, 1891 till 1897.

He is now State Sealer of Weights, Measures and Balances, of the State of Rhode Island, having been appointed February 1st, 1901.

He became a member of the Grand Army of the Republic, by joining Kit Carson Post No. 1, Department of New Mexico, in 1868, and joined Slocum Post, No. 10, Department of Rhode Island by transfer, in 1872, of which post he held the offices of Adjutant and Chaplain; was a charter member of Arnold Post No. 4, Department of Rhode Island, in 1877, of which post he has held the positions of Officer of the Day and Senior Vice Commander; was Chief Mustering Officer, Department of Rhode Island, in 1877 and 1879, and Assistant Mustering Officer in 1890: was a member of the National Council of Administration and a Delegate to the Twentieth National Encampment, held at San Francisco in 1886. Commander of Arnold Post No. 4, Department of Rhode Island, 1897. He was the first president of the California Volunteer Veterans Association, elected at Detroit, Michigan, August, 1891, and has held the office of Secretary and Treasurer since.

He became a member of the Military Order of the Loyal Legion of the United States, Commandery of California. November 10th, 1886. Insignia No. 5065.

He is a member of the Society of California Volunteers: also of the Society of California Pioneers of New England. Is an Honorary Member of the Second Rhode Island Veteran Association; Battery B, Veteran Association: Fourth Rhode Island Veteran Association: and the Fifth Rhode Island, and Battery F. Veteran Association.

d. January 28, 1909, Providence, RI.

"I have always believed that General Carleton wanted me killed, for he put [a] detachment under my command to escort them to the Pima villages, a distance of nearly two hundred miles, and gave me a cavalry detachment of ten men, the worst disciplined ones I ever met. The first night out, when I was encamped at the Point of Rocks, an express arrived from Colonel West, then in command at Tucson, in which I was informed that my prisoners had stated before we left that point, that they would never be taken through alive, and cautioning me to be ever on the alert, or I would not get through. Carleton did not send me for the honor. He was much surprised when I returned safe, but not as much as I was. G. H. P."

JOSEPH F. BENNETT

Brevet Lieutenant Colonel U. S. Volunteers.

The following biographical sketch of this gallant and efficient soldier is taken from the columns of the *Mexican Herald*, published in the City of Mexico, July 9, 1904.

Joseph F. Bennett was born in Putnam County, New York. November 11th, 1839. He received an education afforded by the common schools, and graduated from Millville Academy. Orleans County, New York. In 1849 he accompanied his parents to Janesville, Wisconsin.

In 1858 he emigrated to California and British Columbia going by the Isthmus of Panama, in which countries he was actively engaged in mining until the breaking out of the war when on the call of President Lincoln for 5,000 volunteers from California, in August, 1861, Colonel Bennett aided in raising and organizing the First California Infantry Volunteers enlisting as a private in G company of that regiment. In the winter of 1861 he was made sergeant major of the regiment, and in April 1862, he was commissioned second lieutenant of I company, and assigned by General James H. Carleton as assistant adjutant general of the Column from California at his headquarters in Santa Fe, N. M. Upon the recommendation of General Carleton, and General J. E. West, Lieutenant Bennett was commissioned by President Lincoln, captain and assistant adjutant general United States Volunteers, and was assigned to duty as adjutant general of the district of Arizona. On March, 1864, under orders of the secretary of war [Edwin Stanton], Captain Bennett reported for duty to Major General [William] S. Rosecrans at St. Louis. Missouri, thereafter he participated in the Price campaign and invasion of Missouri in the autumn of that year. During this period, Captain Bennett was breveted major and lieutenant colonel on the same day by the president for "gallant and meritorious services."

In May 1865, Colonel Bennett was sent by General [Grenville] Dodge, then commanding the department of the Missouri, into Arkansas to offer terms of surrender to Brigadier General M. Jeff Thompson, Confederate States Army, and received the surrender of General Thompson and paroled his command, numbering about 9,000. In the summer and fall of 1865, Colonel Bennett accompanied General Dodge in a campaign against the Indians* in the Northwest, at the time of the combined uprising of nearly all of the tribes in the western country. In the winter of 1865, at his own request, Colonel Bennett was ordered to report at his home to await his order of muster-out and was mustered out of the service in June, 1866, having served throughout the [Civil War].

*The Powder River Expedition of 1865 a large punitive operation against the Sioux, Cheyenne, and Arapaho Indians in Montana Territory and Dakota Territory.—Ed. 2016

Colonel Bennett was afterwards commissioned by President [Ulysses S.] Grant, as vice consul to Chihuahua, Mexico, but, having actively engaged in business in New Mexico, declined that appointment. Colonel Bennett had served in many official capacities in his adopted territory as county clerk, clerk of the United States district court, commissioner of the court of claims, United States commissioner and in 1871-72 was a member of the legislative council. He had been identified with many of the leading enterprises in the territory, both private and public, and in May, 1889, was appointed by President Harrison United States Indian agent for the Mescalero Apaches.

Colonel Bennett was married at Las Cruces New Mexico, February 4th, 1864, to Miss Lola Patton, of La Mesilla. They had a family of seven children living as the fruit of their union. Colonel Bennett was a Royal Arch Mason and a member of Philip Sheridan Post, G. A. R., Las Cruces, N. M., and served one term as assistant adjutant general of the Department of New Mexico, Grand Army of the Republic.

Colonel Bennett was appointed vice and deputy consul general of the United States in the City of Mexico in September, 1897, and served as such two years.

He was the first member of the new society of the American colony to die since its organization.

CYRUS H. DE FORREST

First Lieutenant, First Colorado Volunteer Infantry.

Cyrus H. De Forrest entered the service as first lieutenant First Colorado Infantry, and participated with his command in the battle at Apache Pass (or Glorieta) in 1862. He served as aide de camp on the staff of brigadier General James H. Carleton with headquarters at Santa Fe during 1863, 1864, 1865 and 1866. He is now living at Cleveland, Ohio.

GEORGE S. COURTRIGHT

Assistant Surgeon U. S. Volunteers.

George S. Courtright served for three years as post surgeon at Fort Sumner on the Pecos Giver and was stationed there during the time the Navajo Indians were held as prisoners on the Fort Sumner reservation. He was also surgeon for the campaign in the expedition commanded by Brigadier General Christopher Carson [Kit Carson] against the Comanches and Kiowa Indians, and was engaged at the battle of the Adobe Walls, November 25, 1864.

BENJAMIN C. CUTLER

Adjutant First California Volunteer Infantry.

Benjamin C. Cutler entered the service as adjutant of the First California Volunteer Infantry, August 15, 1861. He served with the regiment in that capacity until he arrived in New Mexico when he was appointed by Brigadier General James H. Carleton commanding the expeditionary force, as assistant adjutant general of the Department of New Mexico with the rank of captain, and continued in that position until 1866. His death occurred shortly thereafter and his remains were interred in the National cemetery in Santa Fe.

WASHINGTON L. PARVIN

Captain Company F, First California Volunteer Infantry.

This officer entered the service upon the organization of the regiment at San Francisco, California, August 16, 1861. He resigned November 26, 1862, at Mesilla, Dona Ana county New Mexico. He then returned east and now lives in Washington where for nine years he has been doorkeeper at the War Department.

b. 1825, d. March 15, 1909, interred at Arlington National Cemetery.

JOHN L[UDLOW] VIVEN

Late Brevet Captain U. S. Volunteers.

John L. Viven entered the service in November, 1861, as a sergeant in Company D, First California Volunteer Cavalry. During most of his service he was on duty as a clerk at the department and district headquarters. He was mustered out at Santa Fc, March 15. 1864, to accept a second lieutenant's commission in the First New Mexico

Volunteer Cavalry, and was promoted to first lieutenant March 25, 1865. Honorably mustered out April 19, 1866, at Santa Fe, New Mexico. Was appointed second lieutenant 12th U. S. Infantry February 23, 1866; promoted to first lieutenant April 5, 1866, and appointed regimental quartermaster March 6, 1869, which position he filled to February 28, 1871. Promoted to captain March 31, 1873. Died January 9, 1896. He was breveted captain U. S. Volunteers March 2, 1867, for faithful and meritorious services during the war.

b. *March 5, 1833 NY, d. January 9, 1896, interred at Arlington National Cemetery.*

[JAMES] B. WHITMORE.

Late First Lieutenant First California Volunteer Infantry.

Enlisted August 16, 1861. Immediately appointed sergeant major of the First California Volunteer Infantry. Was appointed second lieutenant of Company A. of the First California Volunteer Infantry, September 5, 1861, and first lieutenant, Company G, First California Volunteer Infantry. October 25, 1862. He was with the company that was ordered to and established Fort McRae at the Ojo del Muerto, the Spring of Death and which was located in what is now called McRae Canyon. This carryon leading from the Tornado del Muerto to the Rio Grande and Fort McRae and the spring are situated about one and one-half miles from the river. There his company did very good service against hostile Apaches. Lieutenant Whitmore was mustered out with the regiment after its completion of service. He committed suicide at Los Angeles, June 21, 1898.

JACOB J. REESE

Sergeant Company C, Fifth California Volunteer Infantry.

Jacob J. Reese served as a sergeant in Company C, Fifth California Volunteer Infantry during his whole term of service. He enlisted in the regiment at its organization in San Francisco and was mustered out after expiration of service in New Mexico. His command was engaged in several skirmishes with the Apaches in which he conducted himself with bravery and coolness he had all the qualities of a good soldier and was very popular among his comrades. He is now spending his old age in peace and quiet in Harrisburg, Pennsylvania.

CHARLES H. WALKER.

First Sergeant Company K, First California Volunteer Infantry.

Enlisted at San Francisco, November 22, 1861, and was assigned to Company K, First California Volunteer Infantry. Was promoted to first sergeant of his company, April 28, 1863. Honorably mustered out November 29, 1864. His record as a soldier is first class. He is now living at Globe, Arizona. He served with the regiment during its entire campaign at stations in Arizona and New Mexico.

b.–?, d.–?

ARTHUR [INGERSOLL] LOCKWOOD

Corporal Company C, First California Volunteer infantry.

Enlisted in the regiment at its organization in San Francisco and served with it during its entire service in Arizona and New Mexico. He was a fine soldier. He is now a resident of San Antonio, Texas, where he has held the office of mayor of the city, and also has been elected several times to the office of alderman.

b. August 21, 1835, NY, d. February 16, 1927.

JULIUS C. HALL

Enlisted at San Francisco, November 9, 1861, and served his full term of enlistment, being mustered out at Fort Union, New Mexico, November 29th, 1864. He was an exemplary soldier and served with his regiment in Arizona and New Mexico. He is now a resident of Wallingford, Connecticut, and an honored and respected citizen enjoying all the comforts of a well spent life.

b. March 22, 1819, NY, d.–?

DAVID DOOLE

Enlisted in Company A, First Regiment California Infantry at San Francisco. August 15th, 1861. He served his full term of enlistment, in the regiment. He was with his company during its campaign in Arizona, and New Mexico. He had served before in the regular army in the Sixth U. S. Infantry, and participated in the expedition to Utah in 1860. He is still alive, hale and hearty and a respected citizen of Mason, Texas.

He is a member of the Fraternity of Ancient Free and Accepted Masons, and has held the highest positions in the lodge in his home town.

b. November 25, 1832, Ireland, d. August 16, 1924

THE END

DISCOVER MORE LOST HISTORY AT BIGBYTEBOOKS.COM

Printed in Great Britain
by Amazon